Original title:
Peach and Passion

Author: Nathaniel Blackwood
ISBN HARDBACK: 978-1-80586-379-3
ISBN PAPERBACK: 978-1-80586-851-4

Petals of Forbidden Bliss

In the orchard where mischief grows,
Fruit hangs low like gossip flows.
We sneak a bite, oh, what a thrill,
Laughing at our own sweet will.

Sticky fingers, what a sight,
Chasing shadows, pure delight.
Juice drips down and stains our clothes,
Like love notes that nobody knows.

Sunkissed Echoes of Affection

Sunshine flirts with every beam,
Awkward winks, a cheeky dream.
A playful dance, we float and glide,
In the warmth, we often hide.

Giggles bubble, hearts entwine,
Life’s zesty twist, oh, how divine!
We toss and turn, like waves that play,
In this saucy game of ‘Stay or sway?’

Savoring the Golden Hour

Golden light, our cheeky muse,
Time to play, no time to snooze.
With every laugh, the world feels bright,
As we twirl in the fading light.

Moments ripe like fruit on trees,
We share our hopes upon the breeze.
Crunchy munchies, sunny smiles,
We collect joy from childhood miles.

Embracing the Essence of Joy

Life's a twist, a silly spin,
With carefree grins, we dive right in.
Every promise, wild and free,
In this frolic, just you and me.

Laughter rings, the world is bright,
Chasing echoes into the night.
A dash of whimsy, a sprinkle of cheer,
In this joyous caper, we have no fear.

Nectar-rich Moments

In the garden where laughter blooms,
Buzzing bees with silly zooms,
Sweet juice drips from every bite,
Chasing squirrels in pure delight.

Sticky fingers and goofy grins,
Rolling in the grass, let the fun begin,
Nature's candy all around,
Laughter echoes, joy unbound.

Silken Touch of Evening

The sun slips low, a golden hue,
Dinner's a mess, what else is new?
Saucy moments, laughter shared,
Stumbling, fumbling—no one cared.

Wine spills greet the warm night air,
Silly stories, none a care,
Ticks and tocks in shades of glow,
Evenings dance with a gentle flow.

Warmth Wrapped in Velvet

Cuddled close in a fuzzy blanket,
Dancing shadows, who needs a banquet?
Popcorn flies, a tasty bait,
Absurdity awaits, can’t be late!

Mirthful giggles shape the night,
Fuzzy socks and goosebumps ignite,
A symphony of clumsy feet,
As chaos and warmth cheerfully meet.

Blossoms of Yearning

Whimsical wishes on a summer breeze,
Ticklish thoughts beneath the trees,
Bulging cheeks from juicy spoils,
Doodle dreams with playful coils.

Giggles hidden in petals bright,
Running wild 'til the sky turns night,
The sweetness lingers, life's delight,
Wrapped in fun, everything feels right.

Dapped Light and Longing

In a garden of giggles, a fruit's delight,
A silly squirrel twirls, what a funny sight!
Sunlight dances, tickling leaves on the floor,
While bees debate who’s the best fruit of all.

Laughter echoes under the shady trees,
As worms pull faces, causing quite the tease.
With every drop, juice spills like a joke,
A sticky situation, yet hearts won't choke.

Sweet Lethe of Young Hearts

Juice drips down chins, a sticky affair,
Young hearts laugh, breathing in summer air.
Frogs croak in sync, putting on their show,
While bugs play concertos in soft undertow.

Catching sweet moments with giggles and grins,
As thoughts turn to crushes, where mischief begins.
A mishap with shadows, they trip and they fall,
In this serenade, they are having a ball.

Shimmering Glow of Afternoon

Breezy whispers float, teasing in the sun,
Each bite brings laughter, oh what silly fun!
The sun winks at lovers under dazzling rays,
As butterflies compete in their fluttery plays.

Sunning on blankets, the giggles grow loud,
While ants steal the fruit from a curious crowd.
Nestled in laughter, forgetting the clock,
These moments, so sweet, are the heart's funny block.

A Harvest of Heartstrings

A basket brimful, with wonders untold,
Jokes wrapped in sweetness, worth more than gold.
A splash in the puddle, mud on the right shoe,
"What a way to end the day!" giggles ensue.

With mischievous grins, the friends share a spree,
In every soft burst, the joy's guaranteed.
Sunset whispers secrets as shadows grow long,
In this silly harvest, they pluck every song.

Entwined in a Sunlit Kiss

In the orchard, they twirl and spin,
Wearing fruit hats, laughing, grinning.
Sweet juice drips, oh what a smell,
Dance in circles, all's well!

Bumblebees buzz, friends join the fun,
With sticky hands, they race and run.
Atop the branches, they take a leap,
Promises made, laughter to keep.

Nature's Lullaby of Affection

Underneath the leafy bow,
Singing silly songs, oh wow!
Caterpillars bob, a funky beat,
With every note, they move their feet.

The sun winks as they wiggle low,
Chasing shadows, swaying slow.
Nature chuckles, sharing its cheer,
A symphony sweet, so crystal clear.

Joy Bathed in Warm Hues

Bouncing along the garden's trail,
With giggles echoing, they won’t fail.
Butterflies wear their best attire,
While twinkling sunlight sets hearts afire.

They munch on snacks, oh what a sight,
Faces smeared with delight, so bright.
Every bite is a grand delight,
As giggles ring out, pure and light.

Savoring the Sun's Embrace

In the park, a picnic is laid,
With funny hats, joyous parade.
Sipping smoothies, making a splash,
With every slurp, they make a crash.

The sun hugs them in rays of gold,
As stories unfold, both daring and bold.
The laughter spreads, a playful tease,
Together forever, living with ease.

Gentle Flickers of Delight

In orchards lush, I start to climb,
A wobbly ladder, a comic mime.
Fruits giggle softly, hiding their hue,
I nearly tumble, a fruit-fueled zoo.

With juices spilling, oh what a mess,
A sticky hand is my new redress.
The drips and drops, a slapstick play,
Nature's own prank, come join the fray!

Euphoria in Every Bite

Biting down on sunlit skin,
A squirt of sweetness, oh what a win!
Crispy crunch meets my happy smile,
It's a fruit frenzy, stay for a while.

Neighbors peek through their fancy curtains,
Wondering why I'm throwing desserts in!
The laughter bubbles as fruit flies sway,
In this cheerful feast, we'll dance and play.

Dreamy Nights and Sweet Fruits

Under the stars, I set the scene,
With frothy drinks, and a taste serene.
Flavors flirt like lovers wide-eyed,
On this fateful dusk, let's take a ride.

The night is winking, a playful tease,
While we scoop goodies among the trees.
A comical chase to catch the last bit,
With laughter ringing, we won’t quit!

The Taste of Things Unspoken

In a silent pact, we lift our spoons,
Caught nibbling secrets under the moons.
Each slice a whisper, a joyful song,
With funny faces, we all belong.

The flavors dance, a secret affair,
Entwined with giggles, we haven't a care.
Unruly crumbs down my chin, oh dear,
But sweet or sour, we live without fear!

Sun-soaked Fantasies

In a land where the sun likes to bake,
Curly tans shine like a funny cake.
People laugh as they slip on a peel,
Oh, the joys that a summer day feels!

Ice cream drips down on a sunny nose,
As kids dance in their grassy clothes.
Lemons compete for the brightest sheen,
While bees buzz around like they’re on sushi cuisine.

Sweetness that Lingers

A fruity wink with every bite,
Their nectar calls like a dance at night.
We giggle as jelly clings to our chins,
Sticky fingers, oh where do we begin?

Friends gather 'round with a fancy board,
Laughing at how they all got floored.
Comedic bites lead to baffled smiles,
Eating our fill, let's stay for a while!

Harvest of Tender Dreams

The orchard whispers sweet little sighs,
As fruit falls gently from sunlit skies.
Squirrels hoot and chase after their snacks,
While laughter erupts with a couple of quacks.

Baskets overflow with our silly stash,
We race to gather, oh what a bash!
Pies form a pyramid, oh what a sight,
Who knew that a bake-off could feel so light?

Garden of Tender Longings

In a garden where giggles cheerfully bloom,
Tiny critters cause creative doom.
Chasing butterflies, the fun won't cease,
Between the petals, we find our peace.

Honey drips on our crooked smiles,
As weeds play dress-up in silly styles.
We skip and hop in this leafy delight,
Only to trip, oh what a funny sight!

Love’s Orchard Awaits

In a grove where laughter grows,
Fruits of whimsy spill and pose.
A bite of glee, a splash of cheer,
Each juicy jest draws us near.

With sticky hands and silly grins,
We chase the fun where joy begins.
A tree of dreams, a shade of play,
In this ripe realm, we'll laugh all day.

Lush Emotions Bursting Forth

A garden filled with silly sights,
Where giggles bloom like gleeful nights.
So juicy sweet, they make us shout,
We dance around, there's no doubt.

With every squish, a joke we share,
Who knew delight could smell so rare?
We plunge our hands into delight,
As laughter stars the brilliant night.

Fragrant Paths to the Heart

On winding trails of zesty fun,
We skip along until we run.
Each step we take, a daffy laugh,
This fragrant route, our silly path.

With whiffs of joy that tickle noses,
A scentsational dance, as anything goes-es.
We'll juggle dreams and throw them high,
In this aromatic maze, we'll fly.

Tasting Sunshine, Feeling Bliss

Sunshine drips like syrup sweet,
On our tongues, it's such a treat.
With every bite, a sunny cheer,
Life's a picnic: have no fear!

We stumble, giggle, and we bask,
In warmth and smiles, no need to ask.
With flavors wild, we twirl and spin,
In this bright world, let the fun begin!

Vibrant Sweetness Unfolded

In a garden of laughter, fruit swings high,
Bouncing colors like tickles that fly.
With a twist and a giggle, it's hard to contain,
Sticky fingers assure we'll never be sane.

Under sunlight, we claim every bite,
Juicy dribbles spark joy, oh what a sight!
One nibble of brightness leads to a spree,
And the world shrinks, just you and me.

Embrace of Ripened Days

Days plump with sunshine, laughter a-plenty,
Forget the diet, today we're quite hungry!
Bashful fruits giggle, as we take our seat,
With squishy delights, oh what a treat!

Mismatched pairs dazzle amid twinkling hues,
A buffet of joy in the tropic blues.
Harmony shifts as we munch and we chime,
Tickling our senses with every good rhyme.

Secrets Hidden in Juiciness

Whispers of sweetness hide in the folds,
Each bite a surprise, as laughter unfolds.
Just when you think you've tasted it all,
A burst of surprise makes you giggle and sprawl.

Mischief lurks in the ripened delight,
Juicy secrets that dance in the night.
With every blush, mischief reigns supreme,
Sips of delight, we're living the dream!

A Dance of Warm Flavors

Spinning around with a splash and a splash,
Tango of tastes, oh what a mad dash!
With a sprinkle of humor, we dive headfirst,
In this flavor fiesta, we’re laughing, not cursed.

Every dance step leads to a giggle or two,
Sassy zest sways, like a playful debut.
Laughter and juiciness, all wrapped in cheer,
Join the parade of flavors, let’s give a loud cheer!

Flesh of Summer's Embrace

In the orchard where laughter grows,
Chasing squirrels, in warm sunlit clothes.
Biting through skin, a juice explosion,
Happiness bursts with the sweetest emotion.

Bees are buzzing, making their rounds,
Sticky fingers and silly sounds.
Dance with the breeze, twirl with a grin,
Life's too short not to dive right in!

Juicy Whispers of Dawn

Morning light spills like a sweet drink,
I ponder the chaos of furry little pinks.
With a splash and a giggle, I take a dive,
Into bright fruit pools where silliness thrives.

Sipping nectar while wearing my hat,
Chattering birds say, 'What's up with that?'
Juices dribble down to my toes,
Who knew mornings could be so gross?

Nectar on the Horizon

As noon approaches, the sun starts to grumble,
I chase rolling fruits, and oh, how they tumble!
A fruit fight erupts, laughter takes flight,
With every squirt, we squeal with delight.

Friends in a frenzy, wearing pulp like crowns,
Squishy sensations replace our frowns.
Who knew juicy orbs could flake so much fun,
Like big blobs of giggles under the sun?

Sweet Heat of Desire

Under the shade of a friendly old tree,
We trade our stories like they're candy for free.
A dab of sweetness, a wink in the air,
Laughter and teasing, we haven't a care.

With flavors igniting and smiles galore,
We squeak and we squawk, demanding more.
In this moment, we all let it be,
Life's a juicy ride, let's roll with glee!

A Meld of Nature and Desire

In a garden where giggles grow,
Laughter dances, sweet and low.
Fruits in clusters, ripe and round,
Tickle your taste buds, joy is found.

A plump surprise rolls down the lane,
Bouncing softly, a fruity game.
Nature’s jest, a juicy fling,
Who knew fruit could make you sing?

With a wink from the sun so bright,
The orchard cheers, what a delight!
Turning blushes into bright smiles,
Life’s a feast, spanning miles.

So let us toast with sticky hands,
To fruity dreams in merry bands.
A mix of flavors, laughs to share,
Nature's fun is everywhere!

Scented Tales of Affection

Whispers float on summer air,
Fragrant tales that love does share.
Perfumed breezes, tickling noses,
In our hearts, a garden grows.

A squashy fruit plops, what a scene,
Squishing thoughts like jellybean.
In this patch of silly dreams,
Everything's sweeter than it seems.

Chasing scents with light-footed grace,
What a funny, fruit-filled race!
Ticks and giggles, all around,
In this orchard, joy is found.

So let’s frolic without a care,
In a fragrant land, oh so rare.
With laughter echoing high above,
We’ll dance through tales of juicy love!

Melodies of Ripened Hearts

Musical notes in sun-ripened hues,
Strumming secrets with fruity views.
In the chorus of summer's cheer,
Sweet surprises are always near.

Bouncy beats like many a fruit,
Rhythms lively, oh how they suit!
With each bite, a burst of sound,
In this orchard, joy is found.

Ripened hearts play silly games,
Singing tunes with fruity names.
Life's a melody, bright and bold,
With laughter echoing untold.

So join the dance with jelly-like shoes,
In a fruity world, there's much to lose.
But in each laugh and silly part,
You'll find the tunes of a ripened heart!

Infusion of Brightness and Affection

A splash of color, what a sight,
Fruits like confetti, pure delight!
Bubbling breezes tickle the vine,
With each giggle, the sun will shine.

Crafting potions in a jar,
Fruitful hugs from near and far.
Juicy dilemmas, woven bright,
With every sip, we feel the light.

Whirling dervish of zest and joy,
Spinning love – oh what a ploy!
Stickiness rules in this funspace,
With cheeky grins on every face.

So let's unite with fruity cheer,
An infusion of giggles, loud and clear.
In the magic of flavors entwined,
Bright love is the treasure we find!

Fragrant Hues of Affection

In the orchard, fruits abound,
Laughter's echo, joyful sound.
Every bite, a giggle sweet,
Dancing feet, a fruity treat.

With a wink, the tree did sway,
Underneath, we play all day.
Sipping juice, we share a grin,
Life's a game, let us begin.

Colorful smiles, laughter bright,
In the sun, we feel just right.
Sticky fingers, playful fun,
Underneath the golden sun.

Brightly painted, hearts a-flutter,
In this bliss, love's light does utter.
Whimsical moments, silly cue,
Together, we're a tasty brew.

A Taste of Love’s Essence

Beneath the boughs, the world seems clear,
Sips of sweetness mix with cheer.
A fruity splash upon our lips,
Giggles burst like fearless ships.

Juice dribbling down our chin,
In this mess, the game begins.
Laughter mingles with each bite,
In this scrumptious, silly fight.

Witty jests in summertime,
Every pun, a fruity rhyme.
Whirling 'round like a spinning top,
In this joy, we never stop.

Frolic through these carefree days,
Joyful hearts in bright sun’s rays.
Morsels shared with glee and glee,
Oh, what fun for you and me!

Sunlit Rapture in the Garden

In the garden, soft and bright,
Colors dance, a pure delight.
Sunkissed laughter, sweetened air,
What a time, without a care.

Chasing shadows, running fast,
Living moments, love amassed.
Lemonade and fruit galore,
Silly games we can't ignore.

Joyful spirit, wild and free,
Dancing with the buzzing bee.
In the sun, our shadows play,
Mirthful hearts, in child’s way.

Petals whisper, secrets beam,
Weaving tapestries of dream.
With each chuckle, hearts ignite,
In this garden, pure delight.

Orchard Serenade of Joy

Under trees that sway and bend,
Silly moments never end.
Tickled taste buds, sweet delight,
What a wondrous, fun-filled night.

Songbirds chirp a playful tune,
Chasing twilight ‘neath the moon.
With each grin, the orchard sings,
Joyful hearts, with feathered wings.

Playful breezes, mischief calls,
Fruity rain, like hidden halls.
Whirl around, a merry chase,
In this dance, we find our place.

Giggling softly, side by side,
In this bliss, our joy can't hide.
Every laugh, a pearly drop,
In this orchard, love won’t stop.

Rubies of the Warmest Sun

In the orchard, laughter sings,
Juicy gems that summer brings.
Silly faces, sticky hands,
Delightful games in sunlit lands.

Bouncing kids with silly grins,
Squirrels plotting their cheeky wins.
With every bite, a squirt of cheer,
Each juicy burst, a laugh to hear.

Chasing shadows, weaving fun,
Stumbling under the golden sun.
Giggles echo, whispers play,
As sticky treasures lead the way.

At dusk, our laughter starts to fade,
With laughing hearts, we felt the raid.
Rubies lost on our shirts and cheeks,
In the end, joy is all we seek.

Aroma of Blissful Encounters

A fragrant breeze swirls in the air,
Bumbling bees with loads to share.
Sweet surprises in every nook,
Each little taste, a well-kept hook.

Oh, what wonders dangling down,
Quirky smiles from all around.
With every whiff, we take a chance,
Follow scent on a merry dance.

Friends and flavors blend and twine,
Silly tales on everybody's line.
Laughter lingers, happy vibes,
Across the field, the joy imbibes.

As night drapes on, we toast with glee,
To every hug and memory.
In sweet aromas, bliss we find,
Life's a feast, tastefully kind.

Lush Harmony in the Orchard

In the grove of laughter's echo,
Bright-green wonders put on a show.
Whimsical shapes and jester hues,
Creating frames for all our views.

Beneath the trees, we spin in whirl,
Twirling like a dizzy pearl.
Sun-kissed cheeks and joyful shouts,
Every moment cheers and doubts.

Pies and games, oh, what a mix,
Hiccups echo with silly tricks.
Capering critters join our play,
In this lush world, we'll dance away.

Evening settles with a sigh,
Starry lights in the velvet sky.
With every giggle and happy song,
In harmony, we all belong.

Licks of Delightful Escape

With every lick, the world unfurls,
Tasty wonders, giggling twirls.
Sundaes topped with chaos reign,
As sticky fingers dart through rain.

In the corner, a funny cat,
Eyes like marbles, chubby fat.
He swipes a scoop from bowls of cheer,
Causing friends to squeal and leer.

Bubbles pop and spoons collide,
Invisible friends on joy's wild ride.
In every drip and splash we spill,
Laughter mingles with the thrill.

As the sun dips low, we shout, hooray!
In splashes of joy, we find our way.
Chasing dreams with sticky glee,
In each sweet lick, we're truly free.

Juicy Whispers in Twilight

In the orchard’s glow, I sip and grin,
A fruit so sweet, it draws you in.
With every bite, I feel the tease,
Like sticky fingers on the breeze.

The squirrels chatter, they’ve found their stash,
I laugh aloud; they make a splash.
Yet here I sit, a sticky foe,
With juice so ripe, it steals the show.

Friends walk by, they shake their heads,
"He’s lost to fruit!" they jokingly said.
But in this bliss, I find my muse,
A zesty life is mine to choose.

Beneath the stars, we laugh and play,
With every bite, we drift away.
In this twilight, we’re young and free,
Chasing sweet dreams under the tree.

Golden Delights in Bloom

Amidst the boughs, a golden glow,
A sight to see, it steals the show.
With plump delights, I make my claim,
I’m just a kid, but feel the fame.

Laughter echoes through the air,
As friends arrive with silly flair.
Each fruity bite ignites the cheer,
A banquet here, bring all your gear!

We juggle fruits, they slip and slide,
A hilarious, sticky joyride.
The laughter’s ripe, as smiles take flight,
In our golden garden, all feels right.

The sun dips low, our giggles soar,
In this bloom, we crave for more.
With each delight, we toast our fun,
Our fruity feast has just begun!

Sunkissed Heartstrings

In the summer haze, we dance and sway,
With cheeks like berries, we laugh and play.
A sip of nectar, oh what a thrill,
Each drop is joy, a sugary spill.

We spin in circles, arms wide and bold,
Chasing the sunshine, we're never old.
With every giggle, we drop our cares,
Fruity flavors hang in the air.

A slip, a slide, oh what a mess!
The fruit's our crown, we wear it no less.
Each juicy jest brings shrieks of glee,
With heartstrings strummed, we sing carefree.

As twilight falls, our laughter rings,
In this sunlit world, our hearts take wing.
Together here, we'll always stay,
With sweetened jewels to light our way.

Orchard of Desires

In a patch of bliss, I found a thrill,
A treasure trove that makes me spill.
With laughter ripe and eyes aglow,
Each fruit's a dream that steals the show.

Friends join in with feigned delight,
"Are you a hero?" in quirky plight.
But as we munch, our worries fade,
In this orchard, our tales are made.

We trade our snacks, a zany deal,
With sticky hands, we squeal and squeal.
A dance of joy beneath the trees,
Each silly moment, just like a breeze.

So here we stand, a fruity crew,
In a world of fun, where dreams come true.
With each plump bite, our hearts ignite,
In this orchard of desires, all feels right.

Forming Bonds Under Boughs

Underneath the leafy shade,
We share a giggle, a fun charade.
Juicy secrets drip from lips,
Like sticky fingers, sweetened tips.

The fruit above seems to conspire,
As we laugh and dance in dry attire.
A friend slips, they make a splash,
In a puddle of soft, squishy stash.

Sunlight filters through the leaves,
Filling our hearts, quite the reprieves.
A bite, a laugh, the juice runs free,
We bond like a syrupy jamboree!

So here we sit in summer's glow,
With fruity treasures in tow.
With each laugh, we make a pact,
Under boughs where life's intact.

Sunset's Embrace on the Skin

The sky blushes, shades of light,
Our giggles echo into the night.
Like sticky fingers, we chase the sun,
In sweet delight, we’re all just fun.

Golden hues decorate our skin,
A sticky kiss, where jokes begin.
We slip on laughter, toss aside cares,
Chasing shadows, meeting glares.

The day retreats, yet spirits climb,
As evening sings its silly rhyme.
We toast to joy, just us and the scene,
A fruity toast, know what I mean?

With each sunset, new tales we weave,
Making memories that we’ll believe.
In fading light, we jest and tease,
Wrapped in warmth, a gentle breeze.

Elixir of the Golden Hour

As daylight drips, we sip and cheer,
An elixir bright, so crystal clear.
With laughter bubbling like a fizzy drink,
Bringing clouds together, don't you think?

In twilight's glow, we raise our cups,
To funny moments, hiccuping pups.
The world feels soft, a silly spree,
With giddy love, let's dance, you and me.

A mix of colors blends at dusk,
We toss a joke, it's a fruity musk.
Each sip brings giggles, a friendly duel,
With friends in tow, we'll break the rule.

So here's to joy, bubbly and bright,
As laughter spills into the night.
May our hours be full of endless cheer,
With every drop, let's toast, my dear!

Echoes of Amber Flavors

Whispers dance on a warm breeze,
With echoes of laughter, we aim to please.
A taste of sweet, in every bite,
Our smiles shine, oh what a sight!

Around the table, we all convene,
Sharing tales fit for the big screen.
Juicy memories, a sticky boon,
As we groove to a fruity tune.

With flavors amber, we toast anew,
Sipping with friends, just me and you.
Every scoop tells a tale of glee,
In our circle, life's meant to be free.

So let's savor those flavors bold,
With each laugh, watch our stories unfold.
In echoes sweet, we create our song,
In this fruity jam, we all belong.

Blossoms of Bursting Hearts

A fuzzy orb hangs on the tree,
With whispers sweet, it calls to me.
I reach up high, but it slips away,
Laughter echoes, it's a fruit play!

Bouncing back, it rolls to the ground,
A train of ants gather all around.
They feast on nectar, so sticky and bright,
I wipe my hands, oh what a sight!

In the breeze, they dance and sway,
Unruly like kids in a big ballet.
Each ripe sun fruit, a jester's prank,
I giggle as juice spills from my tank!

With cherubs smiling from the sky,
They surely see this gooey pie.
What madness in these sunny spheres,
Fruitful ruckus brings us cheer!

Ripened Dreams in Sunlight

In afternoon's glow, a secret waits,
A treasure concealed on garden plates.
It beams with glee, oh what a tease,
Yet rolls away, what a fruit breeze!

I chase it down, the perfect catch,
But alas! It hides under the latch.
A sticky moment, a graze on my arm,
Yet all I can do is laugh at its charm!

Under the sun, joy multiplies,
Citrusy bursts ignite the skies.
I dab the juice on my friend's nose,
And in fits of giggles, the mischief grows!

From shadows, a voice declares the score,
"Life's wild ride just begs for more!"
With sticky fingers and silly smiles,
We munch and crunch for endless miles!

The Allure of Golden Spheres

Behold the marbles, oh what a sight,
Sun-drenched treasures, pure delight.
Round and plump, they sit in a row,
Whispers of sweetness, they steal the show!

With every nibble, a laughter bursts,
Juices dribble, and quirkiness thirsts.
Spinning wildly, they tease and run,
Chasing them down just doubles the fun!

A pie in the sky starts to descend,
With oodles of cream, it comes to mend.
The golden fruits join this merry feast,
As laughter echoes, our joy increased!

A wink from the sun, a nod from the moon,
Let's dance in gardens, let's sing a tune.
For within this joy, we find our dreams,
In every fruit dance, laughter redeems!

Sensual Juices of Paradise

Dripping nectar from the skies,
Wiggly worms with cheeky sighs.
Flavors burst, it’s all a game,
In this juicy world, we’re never the same!

A slip, a slide, on the fruit’s own wall,
A juicy tumble, oh how we fall!
Rosy cheeks, we slip and glide,
Laughter in the air, let joy collide!

As innocent blobs, we make our way,
Through luscious gardens, we laugh and play.
Juicy tales flow like rivers wide,
In our paradise, we take the ride!

With fruits like suns and giggles loud,
Here’s our promise, we stand so proud.
In this silly whirl of flavor's might,
We celebrate life, oh what a delight!

Flavors of Untold Stories

In a garden where sweetness thrives,
A fruit fell down, did somersaults and dives.
Bumblebees buzzed in a jolly dance,
While squirrels plotted a nutty romance.

Lemonade dreams float on the breeze,
Fruits in a debate, 'Who'll take the cheese?'
Jokes about cherries with their round, rosy cheeks,
As giggles of ripeness flow from the creeks.

A citrus clown juggles with zest,
While peaches shyly hide, feeling less blessed.
But laughter erupts from the tree's funny crack,
With birds in boisterous, comedic flack.

So here’s to the fruits that play and tease,
Whispering secrets carried along with the breeze.
With every burst of flavor, joy takes flight,
In a world so merry, every day feels bright.

The Warmth of Amber Days

Amber sunlight drips from the sky,
As giggles bounce like butterflies high.
A silly cat in a sunbeam sprawls,
Dreaming of food while it silently squalls.

Crisp wind plays tricks on hats and hair,
While friends swap tales with exaggerated flair.
Each story ripe, like fruit on the vine,
Turns ordinary days into something divine.

Dancing leaves toss in the seasonal fun,
Chasing after shadows, just like the sun.
Peeking at bugs with a curious grin,
As laughter bubbles up like a warm, fizzy kin.

So gather your friends, share a good pun,
Let the warmth of the day make you feel young.
With smiles that twinkle under the glow,
In this amber moment, let the joy flow.

Honeyed Words and Silken Touch

Whispers of sweetness drift through the air,
Like sticky fingers on a sofa chair.
Giggles erupt from a hidden nook,
As characters plan their next silly look.

A dance of words, each one a treat,
Tickling the palate, oh so sweet!
Smooth like butter, the jokes unfold,
In a tapestry of tales, pure gold.

Sticky notes plastered on the fridge,
With doodles of dreams that tease and smidge.
A splash of humor, a dollop of fun,
Revealing the sunshine after each pun.

With friends gathered 'round, laughter does thrive,
A jester's cap makes the moment come alive.
So savor each giggle, let joy be the crutch,
In this honeyed realm, we all feel the touch.

Harvest Moon and Tender Unsung Melodies

Under the harvest moon's bright glow,
A dance with fruit, just take it slow.
Laughter sparkles, we trip and sway,
Who knew a fruit could lead the way?

Beneath the stars, we juggle delight,
A slippery treat, what a silly sight!
Giggles burst like juice from the core,
We sing off-key, wanting more and more!

The night's alive with our foolish cheer,
As we pluck at dreams, drawing them near.
Sweetness drips as humor spills,
In our orchard of unplanned thrills.

With each bite, a silly tale unfolds,
Of sticky fingers and daring holds.
We chase the night, let laughter ring,
In the harvest's glow, oh what joy it brings!

Fuzzy Dreams of Summer

In fuzzy dreams of summer's grace,
We dance around in a fruity embrace.
Each splash of juice births a grin,
Too much fun, where do I begin?

The air is thick with silly air,
A fruit fight breaks out, we don't care!
Rolling on the grass, oh what a sight,
Getting sticky under morning light.

We play tag with the sun, oh so bright,
Chasing shadows with all our might.
Juicy giggles fill the warm breeze,
In the chaos, we find our ease.

We craft our crowns with leaves and drinks,
Sippin' on laughter, don't you think?
Fuzzy dreams lead us further away,
The taste of summer forever will stay!

Luscious Embrace of Dawn

As dawn breaks with a colorful sigh,
We're mixing juice while passing by.
Luscious mornings invite a prank,
A splash of color from the tank!

Every sip brings a giggle out loud,
"Did you steal mine?" I shout to the crowd.
The table's a mess, with spills galore,
In this fruity feast, who could ask for more?

We chase the sun across the green,
In a world of whims, we're unseen.
With each burst of flavor in the air,
Our laughter lingers without a care.

Can you catch joy like you catch a breeze?
With each silly game, we aim to please.
In the morning's light, let's lay and play,
Embraced by laughter, let's seize the day!

Sweet Nectar on the Breeze

Sweet nectar floating through the air,
With every breeze, a prank we share.
We chase the wind, our footsteps light,
In a game of taste, we feel so bright!

Tasting joy like it's a sweet treat,
Dancing on tiptoes, oh how neat!
A drop here, a splash there, what a mess!
Our laughter echoes, love's sweet caress.

Flavors mingle with giggles galore,
We dive into fun, craving more.
Each twirl and spin, a story told,
In the nectar's warmth, we're feeling bold.

The world is ripe with silly delight,
In our orchard of dreams, we take flight.
So let's raise a glass to joyful times,
With sweet nectar swirling, life's in our rhymes!

Juicy Secrets Beneath Leaves

In a garden where squirrels parade,
Lies a treasure, a tiptoe charade.
With each secret bite, laughter ensues,
As critters debate on the best kind of dues.

Round the trees friends gather, quite bold,
Sharing whispers of tales long retold.
Each munch brings a giggle, a grin,
As sticky fingers dance in a playful spin.

Under the shade, the mischief brews,
With sun-kissed cheeks, no time to lose.
The fruit may drop, but spirits won’t fall,
As giggles echo, calling one and all.

So come, join the fun, let’s make a feast,
Laughter our banner, joy never ceased.
In a world where sweetness reigns supreme,
Together we’ll create the silliest dream.

Sweet Liberation of Spirit

A whimsy floats on the gentle breeze,
Where laughter leaps and wiggles with ease.
With sweet nectar spilling in cheer,
Every giggle rings loud, oh dear!

Frivolity dances on fruit-laden vines,
As bees join the party, forming new lines.
With a swift little bounce and a hop,
We fling away worries and let laughter pop.

Beneath a canopy of foliage, we play,
Where time skips and hops, come what may.
In this realm of delight, let's sway and spin,
Freedom is sweeter than the tartest skin.

So let's raise a toast, to silliness grand,
To the laughter and freedom that life has planned.
With spirits unchained, we eat and we sing,
In this zesty dance, let our joy take wing.

The Glow of Enchantment

Under a shimmer of stars at dusk,
We revel in magic, as odd as a husk.
Glowworms giggle, in a line they tread,
While grasshoppers serenade, in green they're bred.

Bright orbs of sweetness hide close by,
Revealing delights as the night hums a sigh.
Tickled by whispers, the laughter ignites,
With every juicy morsel, our joy takes flight.

Sipping on dreams from goblets of cheer,
Every sip shared, makes worries disappear.
Floating on whims, with a chuckle we boast,
About the curious creatures we cherish the most.

So here's to enchantment, under moon's gentle sway,
With joy as our compass, we'll laugh our way.
In the heart of this night, let our giggles unfurl,
For every sweet moment's a wondrous whirl.

Serenading the Sun through Softness

A bright morning calls, with a wiggle and spin,
Birds sing in harmony, where shall we begin?
With sunbeams that tickle and curl around feet,
We bound into laughter, oh, what a treat!

Pies of sunblush, on the porch they rest,
While squirrels audition for the role of the jest.
With mischievous grins, they plot and they plan,
Crafting a feast that would baffle a man.

Each slice is a giggle, each crumb a delight,
As we munch through the warmth of this buttery light.
Belly laughs echo from kitchen to yard,
In this soft serenade, life's never too hard.

So, let's celebrate warmth with a whimsical cheer,
Sharing sweet moments, together we're here.
With sun-kissed delight, may our laughter ignite,
This silly little gathering, a pure-hearted sight.

Euphoria Wrapped in Silk

In a world where laughter blooms,
Chasing joy in bright costumes.
Silly dances, a cheerful spin,
Wrapped in silk, we laugh and grin.

The fruit is sweet, a juicy tease,
We nibble close with playful ease.
Giggles echo from cheek to cheek,
A fruity joke, hide and seek.

Like clowns we juggle, flavors collide,
In every burst, pure joy can't hide.
With every bite, the world feels light,
In this fun feast, it feels so right.

So join the dance, let worries slip,
On this sweet ride, take a trip.
Wrapped in silk, with laughter near,
Life’s fruity punch brings endless cheer.

Forbidden Fruits of Love

Beneath the tree where secrets grow,
I plucked the fruit, oh how it glows.
A rogue delight, a sinfully sweet,
With every bite, my heart skips a beat.

We share a grin on this wild ride,
As flavors burst, we toss aside.
The taste of mischief lurks in air,
A secret crush, with cheeky flair.

Oh what a scene, this tasty game,
With every nibble, we fan the flame.
Laughter spills, a playful chase,
In this love fest, we find our place.

So take my hand, let's cause a stir,
Amongst the fruits, our laughter purrs.
Forbidden flavors, joy's delight,
In this sweet union, hearts take flight.

The Soft Glow of Twilight Yearnings

At dusk, when shadows start to play,
We sip on dreams, let worries sway.
Twilight whispers, teasing our fate,
In this soft glow, love can't wait.

Craving laughter like glowing fire,
With every joke, we spark desire.
A giggle here, a wink, a cheer,
In twilight's hush, we lose all fear.

With sweet delights, our voices rise,
Chasing stars in the velvet skies.
Fruits of whimsy, feel the breeze,
In every giggle, life's a tease.

So let's wander, in this soft dance,
With shared sweet bites, we take a chance.
In twilight's soft, passionate glow,
Our hearts entwined, just let it flow.

Ripe Moments in Twilight's Grip

Under the moon, the fruit hangs low,
A ripe delight, the world aglow.
With each sweet nibble, laughter spills,
In twilight's grip, we find our thrills.

Oh what a scene, with colors bright,
We chase the giggles 'til the night.
The taste of fun, a secret blend,
Where every moment feels like a trend.

A playful dance beneath the stars,
In this sweet joy, we drop our guards.
With laughter ringing through the air,
Twilight's charm is beyond compare.

So let's indulge in this sweet spree,
In every bite, pure ecstasy.
With ripe moments that never stop,
In twilight's grip, we laugh and hop.

A Hug from Nature’s Lab

In a garden of fruits, oh what a sight,
The roundest of orbs, they giggle with delight.
They rustle and tease, those cheeky little seeds,
In sun-kissed attire, fulfilling our needs.

With whispers of sweetness that make you grin,
They argue in flavors, each wanting to win.
One claims to be juicy, another so fine,
In this fruity theatre, all take their time.

A jellybean cousin makes mischief anew,
With a squishy embrace, it just might stick to you.
The nectar so rich, it’s slippery fun,
This zesty romance has only begun!

So pluck up the courage, don that fruity crown,
Join in the laughter, let nothing weigh down.
For in this lab of nature, we frolic and play,
Where each fruity hug will brighten your day.

Colors of Amorous Temptation

In the rainbow of fruits, a palette so bold,
Each color a story, not yet been told.
Reds hit the stage with a wink and a grin,
While yellows and greens all prepare for a spin.

There's blush on the cheeks, oh what a sight,
As oranges jive with the berries at night.
With juices a-dripping, they stain every dress,
Leaving laughter behind, oh what a sweet mess!

The dappled delights dance with whimsical flair,
Twirling around without a single care.
As flavors collide like a slapstick show,
In this fruity ballet, the laughter will flow.

So gather your friends for this colorful chase,
Entwined in the laughter, we'll all find our place.
Forget all your worries, dive into the spree,
For in this wild romp, we're all fruity glee!

Velvet Paths to the Heart

On paths made of velvet, in sunshine so bright,
The fruit-folk are dancing, what a silly sight!
With flirty green leaves whispering low,
They egg on each other like a comedy show.

A curvy delight rolls past with a tease,
Pleading for giggles, a flirty breeze.
The ones with the fluff swear they're magic in hand,
Casting laughter spells across the land.

Between playful banters, the juices will flow,
Drawn to the sweetness of this wacky glow.
As flavors collide in a ticklish embrace,
We'll wander together in this fruity place.

So follow the trails where the quirks come alive,
Let the velvet connections remind you to thrive.
For in this whimsical patch of delight,
We'll burst into laughter and dance through the night.

The Essence of Golden Cheeks

Oh, those golden cheeks, how they wiggle and sway,
In gorgeous confusion, they brighten the day.
With merry little giggles that spark and delight,
They promise a taste, both juicy and bright.

They flirt with the breeze, as if on a dare,
While the sun paints the sky with a ripe, warm glare.
Poking fun at the world with a mischievous twinkle,
Each bite a burst of fun, make your tongue crinkle.

The nectar drips down, a playful cascade,
With every sweet taste, our doubts start to fade.
In this orchard of joy, no frowns will escape,
As we dive into laughter, each little fruity shape.

So gather your joy, let your worries release,
With those golden delights, embrace fun and peace.
For in this round banquet where flavors unite,
We'll dance in the sweetness, a marvelous sight.

The Language of Luscious Fruits

In sunny orchards, giggles bloom,
Chattering fruits break the quiet gloom.
A cheeky pear tells a tale so tall,
While cherries laugh, bouncing off the wall.

The naughty figs play hide and seek,
With plums so round, they barely speak.
Lemons toss jokes, tart and bright,
A fruit fiesta, pure delight!

Oh, what a party, this fruity show,
Mangoes dance with a swaying flow.
Bananas slip and slide down vines,
Dancing with laughter like silly lines.

Every fruit has a story to share,
In this wacky world of ripe affair.
So grab a snack, come join the fun,
Where jokes taste better when shared by one!

Irresistible Sweetness at Dusk

As twilight whispers, sweetness calls,
Juicy delights line up in stalls.
A cheeky apple, tart yet bright,
Bids goodnight with a wink of light.

Grapes giggle as they dangle low,
Chasing shadows in a glossy row.
Toffee-coated apricots prance,
Tempting all in a silly dance.

There's a berry bash beneath the moon,
With strawberries crooning a fruity tune.
Peaches poke fun, all fuzzy and round,
While limes tell stories without a sound.

And under the stars, the flavors blend,
Tickling our senses like an old friend.
At dusk, the sweetness fills the air,
In this fruity carnival, beyond compare!

Emotions Ripening in Time

In the orchard of thoughts, feelings grow,
Some ripe with laughter, some taut with woe.
Bananas smirk, as they peel away,
While berries blush at what they might say.

Tomatoes rumble, red with surprise,
As cucumbers share tales of their fries.
A space where emotions can freely flow,
Makes the juiciest scenes of life's show.

Peppers sizzle with zest and flair,
Spilling secrets in the evening air.
Cherries giggle, bursting with zest,
While lemons ponder which joke is best.

Time in the garden does pass by slow,
As feelings mix like a gourmet show.
With every bite, a flavor divine,
The bowl of emotions is all so fine!

The Ripple of Juicy Fantasies

Rippling dreams swirl like fresh-squeezed juice,
In a world where flavors break all the truce.
Pineapples crown fantastic affairs,
While raspberries chuckle, naughtier glares.

Watermelons burst with giggles galore,
Sliding down slopes with a juicy roar.
Coconuts chuckle, teasing the breeze,
While donuts roll by, just to appease.

Every twist and turn, a fruity delight,
As joy bounces in the soft moonlight.
Bunches of dreams hang heavy and sweet,
Making every gathering a charming treat.

So come take a sip of this fun-filled brew,
Where juicy fantasies await for you.
With laughter and fruit mixing divine,
Every moment ripens, simply sublime!

Irresistible Savor of Moments

A juicy byte, oh what a tease,
Fruits in hand, we smile with ease.
Your laughter bursts like fizzy fizz,
Dripping sweetness, oh what a whiz!

We stroll about, so carefree and light,
Slipping on juice, oh what a sight!
Chasing flavors, we dance and twirl,
Sweets in our pockets, watch us swirl!

Every bite's a giggle, a cupcake cheer,
Sticky fingers, but we don't care here!
With winks and nibbles, we let out a shout,
Life's a party, without a doubt!

So let's dive in, with zest and glee,
In this fruit fest, you and me!
Wrap me in flavors, give me a grin,
In this sweet moment, let the fun begin!

Tapestry of Warmth and Light

A garden blooms with quirky flair,
Bouncing bugs and squirrelly air.
Bring on the warmth, let's sing and sway,
We'll barbecue bliss, oh what a day!

With each soft bite, a giggle spills,
And laughter echoes upon the hills.
Like sunshine in jars, we're bright and bold,
Stories unfold with flavors untold!

Wobbling fruit, such silly treats,
Made for munching with our two left feet.
Jumping around like springtime kids,
We savor life's candy, the joy it bids!

So gather 'round, don't miss the fun,
Under this light, we're never done.
Sun-soaked moments we won't forget,
In this tapestry, we're all set!

Charmed by the Fruitful Glow

In the orchard, jokes take flight,
We pluck and snack till the stars are bright.
Quotes from squirrels, giggles all around,
In this fruity world, joy abound!

Juicy wonders, a messy affair,
Sticky cheeks, without a care.
We trade our secrets, share our dreams,
In this playful feast, life gleams!

Bursting flavors, laughter spills,
So many choices, it gives us thrills.
Fruity treasures, we gobble and grin,
With every munch, let the fun begin!

Under leafy umbrellas, we play the day,
With hearty chuckles, we sing away.
Charmed by the glow, together we sway,
In this fruity laughter, let's forever stay!

Essence of Blissful Togetherness

In the kitchen, chaos on display,
Chopping and mixing in a playful way.
We tickle the taste buds, add a dash of cheer,
Creating a mess, let's hold dear!

With every toss, we swirl and dance,
Harvesting joy in this merry romance.
Sprinkles of laughter, a pinch of silly,
Baking our dreams, oh how we're really!

The aroma wafts, we can't help but sneak,
Filling our souls with joy when we peak.
In this colorful kitchen, together we stand,
Crafting the sweetness, hand in hand!

So let's raise a toast to these fruity days,
With giggles and glances, in so many ways.
In this essence of life, we find our bliss,
With each tasty moment, it's love that we kiss!

Harvesting Sweetness from Shadows

In the garden where giggles grow,
Beneath the leaves, secret winds blow.
Plucking jokes from branches high,
Sweetness ripe, oh me, oh my!

Squirrels dance with gleeful flair,
Stealing snacks without a care.
We laugh at their daring munching spree,
As fruity treasures go missing, whee!

Sunlight winks through leafy green,
Tickling my toes, a playful scene.
With every bite, a grin appears,
Juicy chuckles kissed with cheers.

So here we frolic, nature’s jest,
Rustling leaves, we’re truly blessed.
In shadowed harvests, smiles ignite,
Funny moments bloom in light.

The Warmth of Tender Touches

A gentle nudge, a playful poke,
Laughter bubbles, it’s no joke.
Fingerlings dance in sunny rays,
Silly games fill up our days.

A soft embrace, like fuzzy vines,
Tickle fights and jolly signs.
We share a smile, then burst with glee,
Nuzzling close, just you and me.

In this warmth, the world seems bright,
Every hug feels just so right.
With every squeeze, our spirits lift,
Joy's the best, our favorite gift!

So let’s wrap up in giggles tight,
Funny moments spark delight.
In tender touches, we find bliss,
A sweet connection, a happy kiss.

Slices of Heaven in Every Kiss

A peck, a smack, a giggly cheer,
Each little touch draws us near.
Our lips unleash a burst of fun,
Like candy clouds beneath the sun!

Messy bites and fruity swirls,
Sticky fingers, playful whirls.
With every kiss, a fruity sound,
Joy spills out, all around!

We giggle like it's our first time,
Tasting sweetness, oh, sublime!
Each mischievous smooch, a delight,
In silly moments, hearts take flight!

So let's devour this happy bliss,
With every silly peck, a kiss.
In slices shared, our laughter bliss,
Finding heaven in every kiss.

Radiance of Heartfelt Cravings

A hunger stirs, for joy we seek,
Craving laughter, cheek to cheek.
With every nibble, smiles unfold,
Tasty tales from gardens bold.

Each bite flings joy like confetti,
Funny cravings, nothing petty.
We munch on dreams and giggles sweet,
Finding bliss in every treat.

With silly flavors, oh what fun,
Devouring joy, we spark and run.
For every chuckle, every cheer,
Hearts illuminate, bright and clear.

So gather round, let's feast tonight,
On heartfelt musings, pure delight.
In radiance, our joys collide,
With cravings met and smiles wide.

Sweet Temptation on the Breeze

A fruit so soft, it winks at me,
With every nibble, I lose my key.
Juice drips down like summer rain,
Tickling my nose and causing me pain.

Round and rosy, a cheeky grin,
Rolling on the grass, I'm diving in.
Biting its skin, a dance with fate,
My diet? Well, I'm sure it's late.

With each sweet taste, I'm feeling bold,
Belly laughs from stories told.
Who needs a diet, what a tease!
Got caught up in this juicy breeze.

Some say it's just a silly fruit,
But look at me, in a furry suit!
Dancing with seeds and sticky threads,
My life just turned to fruity spreads.

The Color of Longing

A blush of skin, so ripe and round,
Craving the sweetness that's always found.
Each bite, I giggle and roll my eyes,
Why does it taste like summer skies?

Painting my tongue in tones so bright,
So bright that even the sun takes flight.
Stealing glances, can't hold it back,
Like sneaky squirrels on a fruity track.

I summon friends for a wild spree,
Fragrant feasts as wild as can be.
Their laughter rings, so joyous and free,
Who knew a fruit could bring such glee?

With every slice, our jokes collide,
Sticky fingers, can't let it slide.
"Oh, share!" I plead with sauce on my cheek,
This flavor festival is far from bleak.

Warmth Beneath the Orchard

In the shade, the laughter flows,
The fruit parade is how it goes.
I spot my treasure, it’s plump and round,
Below the branches, happiness found.

I leap and twirl, like a carefree sprite,
This golden charm is pure delight.
How many dances for one small bite?
It’s a comical, joyous, cheeky sight.

A juggle and toss, then in it goes,
Juicy contrast to all my woes.
Giggles erupt, seeds take flight,
Nothing like this to bring pure light.

So here’s to fun, in the soft sun glow,
Where every laugh, it steals the show.
Embrace the mess, have no fear,
For in this orchard, joy is near.

Luscious Secrets in Every Bite

Beneath the skin, a world so sweet,
Each cozy nook hides a tasty treat.
With every chomp, laughter shines,
Can't help but pull all the right lines.

I prance around, a fruity thief,
Wearing juice like a badge of belief.
Friends join in for a grand buffet,
Oh, the fun we'll find today!

The squirrels giggle, the birds just cheer,
For they know the joys of the nearby sphere.
I take my bite, a playful cheer,
"More fruit, less worry!" rings clear.

So here's to chaos, with every taste,
There's no such thing as a moment waste.
With sticky hands and wild delight,
We'll feast together, morning till night.

www.ingramcontent.com/pod-product-compliance
Lightning Source LLC
Chambersburg PA
CBHW070304120526
44590CB00017B/2553
9781805868514